this old man's harmless fancy; for having in a kindly way done homage to a man who all agree did naught but kindly things?

In Maeterlinck's *Pelleas et Melisande,* Arkel, the venerable King of Allemonde, contemplating the harsh cruelties of man, remarks:

"If I were God, I should pity the hearts of men."

Perhaps—who knows?—to our venerable Emperor Norton came a like compassionate realization of man's inhumanity to man. Perhaps to his half-curtained mind there was revealed the pitiful sense of the measureless pathos of human destiny—its darkening twilights at the end of all delight; its dying echoes, its mystery and its inescapable end. Perhaps for him, through the strange potency of his dream, that which to those about him went unnoticed, became eventful and revealing. And perhaps he saw from behind the veil—much clearer than did those about him—that, as some ancient said: "The circling world is like a dream, but on awakening it becomes too unreal to contemplate."

association, first vice president California Historical Society.

2:50—Address, "Emperor Norton and His Times," George H. Barron, vice president of the association, and past grand historical of the Native Sons of the Golden West.

3:10—Vocal Selection, the Olympic Club of San Francisco.

3:20—Farewell, William Penn Humphries, past master of Occidental Lodge F. & A. M. (Emperor Norton affiliated with this lodge August 21, 1854.)

3:30—Selection, Municipal Band.

3:40—Unveiling of the monument by Fred S. Moody, treasurer of the association.

3:45—Placing of wreaths. (1) By Mayor Angelo Rossi in behalf of the citizens of San Francisco. (2) By Judge Charles A. Shurtleff, president of the Society of California Pioneers. (3) By Allen L. Chickering, president of California Historical Society.

3:55—Salute, Third Battalion, 159th Infantry, C.N.G., Major George Browning, commanding.

4:00—Taps, San Francisco Post American Legion, Raye Gleeson, commander."

Though almost sixty years have passed since the death of Emperor Norton, in San Francisco there yet remains—discernible to all whose eyes see more than bald exteriors—the nimbus of this kingly man, who, in a life of courtly pretense, lived less in league with sham than many a man who scorned him for his child-like vagaries.

And who today will not say that San Francisco is a little finer—a little warmer of heart and nobler of soul—for having in those far-gone years humoured

the spirit of him did not pass. The spirit of him, and of the homage paid him by the City of St. Francis, lived on.

That spirit still lives. On June 30, 1934—fifty-four years after the Emperor's death—San Francisco set aside a day to pay him fresh and further tribute. Said the San Francisco *Chronicle* of that date:

"San Francisco today does what no other city on earth could or would attempt.

"This city by the Golden Gate pauses long enough, in these sorely troubled times, to pay homage to the memory of an emperor who was no emperor, except in his imagination; to a ruler who was no ruler, except in his harmless pretentions; to a king who was no king, except to two nondescript dogs which followed him about the streets of early-day San Francisco as his sole retinue; to a regal splendor that was a complete, but lovable, sham.

"For today, with pomp and ceremony, San Francisco inters in Woodlawn Memorial Park at Colma all that remains of 'Emperor' Norton I, 'Emperor of all the United States and Protector of Mexico.'

"The city turned out 30,000 strong to pay tribute to him when he died January 8, 1880. He was given a public funeral, the city being draped in mourning, and he was interred in the old Masonic Cemetery.

"Now the Emperor Norton Memorial Association will pay a tribute to the 'Emperor.'

"The program follows:

2:30—Selection, Municipal Band.

2:40—Address, Ernest A. Wiltsee, president of the

procured, when it arrived at the place Norton was dead.

"On the reeking pavement, in the darkness of a moonless night under the dripping rain, and surrounded by a hastily gathered crowd of wondering strangers, Norton I, by the grace of God, Emperor of the United States and Protector of Mexico, departed this life. Other sovereigns have died with no more of kindly care—other sovereigns have died as they have lived with all the pomp of earthly majesty, but death having touched them, Norton I rises up the exact peer of the haughtiest King or Kaiser that ever wore a crown. Perhaps he will rise more than the peer of the most of them. He had a better claim to kindly consideration than that his lot 'forbade to wade through slaughter to a throne and shut the gates of mercy on mankind.' Through his harmless proclamations can always be traced an innate gentleness of heart, a desire to effect uses and a courtesy, the possession of which would materially improve the bitterful living princes whose names will naturally suggest themselves."

The funeral of Emperor Norton was said to have been the largest ever held in San Francisco. Flags were hung at half-staff throughout the city; public offices, stores and other business houses were closed, and a procession of more than 30,000 people, including hundreds of children, took four hours to pass the Emperor's bier.

* * * *

So passed from the earthly scene the mortal form of Norton I, America's first and only Emperor. But

California Street, was going up California Street immediately behind the Emperor, saw him fall, and hastened to aid him. With the assistance of others who quickly arrived, the Emperor was placed in a sitting posture on the wet pavement and his back supported against the wall of the corner house. His speechlessness and his head fallen forward on his breast indicated to the rapidly gathering crowd, every one of whom knew him and knew him to be highly temperate, that something serious had befallen him and the police officer on the beat hastened for a carriage to convey him to the City Receiving Hospital. Speedily as the hack had been

old Emperor the crowning event of his kindly reign. The exact date of it is lost in the dimness of old men's memories, but it has been placed by some in the year 1879.

If so, it was probably Emperor Norton's last public appearance. For on the evening of January 8, 1880, as he was walking up California Street on his way to a debate of the Hastings Society at the Academy of Sciences, the Emperor was stricken with apoplexy and died before medical aid could be obtained.

Of his death, a San Francisco newspaper of January 9, 1880, had this, in part, to say:

"Last night at 8:15 Joshua Norton, universally known, and known almost only as Emperor Norton, died suddenly in this city. The similar death of the first citizen of San Francisco, or the highest municipal officer of the city, would not have caused so general a sensation as that of the harmless old man whose monomania never distorted at least a heart which was wholesome, and hardly affected a mind which had once been of the shrewdest, other than in the method of his sovereignty of the United States and Protectorate of Mexico. He had started from Kearny Street up California Street, with the intention of occupying a seat in the rooms of the Academy of Sciences during the debate of the Hastings Society. Almost as he reached the East line of Dupont Street on the south pavement of California he halted for a moment, then staggered forward, halted again and then fell prone on the sidewalk. Wm. Proll, doing business at 537

This man read the proclamation and was at once struck with the novelty and the nobility of the Emperor's proposal. "Why not," he asked himself, "do what the Emperor orders, and do it in the Emperor's name?" Whereupon, he proceeded to confer with his business associates throughout the city, and they, too, immediately fell in with the idea. So a committee was formed, and a score of busy San Francisco merchants, lawyers, doctors, etc., went to work with a will; with the result that the Emperor's noble idea became a beautiful reality. The tallest fir tree ever seen in San Francisco was put up in the center of Union Square, and with its long ropes of tinsel, and its thousands of candles, it made an impressive and a lovely sight.

It was a notable occasion, and one long-remembered. The city's finest band played Christmas music, and a chorus of a hundred voices sang Christmas carols; while a score of busy Kris Kringles gave out thousands of bags of candy and fruit and nuts to the assembled children. And hard by the big Christmas Tree, on a red and green throne, sat Emperor Norton, wearing a new uniform which the Committee had provided; beaming and smiling and waving to the children as they marched by and called out their greetings to him. He was so happy he could scarcely contain himself, and so excited that when it came time to go, he had to be helped down and into the carriage the Committee had hired to take him home.

This public festival in celebration of the birth of the Christ Child may well have been to the kindly

taken over by his host, friend and benefactor, the owner of the Eureka Lodging House on Commercial Street, to be run by the latter as an Imperial caravansery under the Emperor's Imperial patronage. As the story goes, when the Palace Hotel proprietor, after considerable entreaty from Norton I, refused to comply with this request, the Emperor got out a stern proclamation ordering the Chief of Police to clear the hotel of the proprietor and "all his insubordinate seneschals."

Fortunately, with this proclamation, as with all his others, the Emperor did not further concern himself. Once a proclamation was issued he evidently expected it to be self-enforcing. At least, he promptly forgot it, and went on to other affairs. Which may have been one reason that he enjoyed such a long and untrammelled reign.

Another story which has come down to us without benefit of the credentials of authenticity, but which has persisted nevertheless, is the one concerning a public Christmas Tree and celebration held in Union Square at the Emperor's instigation.

As usual, the Emperor introduced the idea through one of his famous Imperial proclamations; which, as was his custom in such matters, he circulated among the city's larger business firms.

It so happened that one of these chanced to fall into the hands of a prominent San Francisco merchant—a man who long had known Emperor Norton and liked him, and who on several occasions had cheerfully paid one of his Imperial "levies."

There are a good many stories about Emperor Norton which are apocryphal. In the nature of things this is only natural. He was a picturesque, if not a picaresque, character, and around such persons grow up all sorts of anecdotes—some true, some false, and some in which truth and falsity are blended. Moreover, as time passes, and the memories of eye-witnesses grow dim, the two attributes tend more and more to merge inextricably.

One such story, which may be true or false, but which seems fairly plausible, tells of the Emperor, in a moment of furious temper, having smashed with his heavy cane a large glass window in a Kearny Street store. The provocation to this display of imperial wrath was the appearance in the window of a caricature of the Emperor, who was pictured standing before a free lunch table. Beside him were his two dogs, Bummer and Lazarus, looking up expectantly at their master. This satire upon his predilection for free lunch counters so incensed Norton I that he raised his cane and demolished the glass.

Proof though this may be that the Emperor was "only human after all"; when one contrasts the light penalty he inflicted, with punishments today meted out in certain lands for any slight show of *lese majesty,* the Emperor's benignity and broadmindedness is the more apparent.

Another anecdote which must be put down as apocryphal is the account of the Emperor's alleged attempt to force out the proprietor of the Palace Hotel, in order to permit that world-famous hostelry to be

Emperor Norton was an excellent conversationalist. Having free access to all libraries and reading rooms, he kept well posted and talked readily and intelligently on any subject. His scientific knowledge, though somewhat mixed, was considerable, and he

was noted for his wide and ready knowledge of history. He liked grand opera, but was especially fond of the weightier dramas of the day, and attended the theatres frequently—being passed without question to all performances. So far as we know he did not care for professional sports, perhaps considering them beneath the dignity of an Emperor.

not most of the recommendations of Norton I, were intensely practical and altogether desirable. And from this standpoint he was eminently more entitled to rule an Empire than were Nero or Caligula, however much he may have lacked their royal lineage. His was never the role of "fiddling while Rome burned," and his innate kindliness and broad-mindedness, of which he gave so many notable manifestations, was a trait that might well be emulated by kings and commoners the world over today.

* * * *

Although Emperor Norton was opposed to female suffrage, and would have been shocked into incoherence by today's spectacle of women rattling around in public offices much too big for them, he was no woman-hater; not by any means. On the contrary, woman in her proper sphere he much esteemed and admired; and was never so pleased as when he was the recipient of a fair lady's smile. We are told that he believed many of the city's belles to be deeply in love with him; a conviction which the receipt of numerous tender missives, written on dainty perfumed note paper did much to solidify. It is said that at times he was even disposed to forget diplomatic exchanges and other high matters of State, in order to attend to this much more intimate and personal correspondence with the "reigning belles" of San Francisco. In this, it is just possible that he was more akin to certain crowned heads of his and other days, than could be judiciously admitted, *officially*.

of them—a bag of candy or oranges or nuts; a top; a horn; a pencil; a tablet; a slate, or some other trinket sure to gladden a youngster's heart. And if, about this time, he levied an extra one of his "Special Assessments" you knew very well where its proceeds went —to many of these children Emperor Norton was the only Santa Claus they had ever known.

In accordance with his unshakable belief that he was an Emperor, of equal rank and power with any European reigning monarch, Emperor Norton's main purpose in life was to administer properly his dominions, and to do everything possible to promote the prosperity and general well-being of his subjects. His diplomatic relations were carefully considered, and he acknowledged freely that he profited by closely observing the progress or decline of other nations, using their experience in his home policy.

He claimed to have reconciled the French and the Prussians, and to have arranged the treaty of peace between them at the end of the Franco-Prussian War. He also insisted that our own Civil War was terminated through his intercession, and was often known to declare that but for his wise counsel the Union might not have been preserved.

The newspapers of the day were usually good-natured enough to humour Emperor Norton's pretenses and whims. Frequently they published his proclamations, many of which, as has been remarked, made proposals which were thoroughly sane and entirely worthy of being effectuated. For all the grandiose language in which they were couched, many, if

demanding, ordering civic improvements—better fire protection; an adequate water system; macadam instead of cobblestone streets; more street cars; better lighting; a bigger post office; a new city hall; and, incredible as it may seem, *a bridge across the Bay to Oakland!*

The last, in fact, was probably his pet obsession in the latter years of his "reign." He issued many "Imperial Proclamations" proposing it, and, finally, one in which he *ordered* it "built without delay." This was accompanied by his hand-drawn sketch of the span; and, believe it or not, the San Francisco terminal of the present mighty structure is within a block or two of the site he designated!

The Emperor was never happier than when surrounded by a group of children. He always had a supply of peppermint lozenges, which he dispensed generously; and he allowed the youngsters to play with his dogs, Bummer and Lazarus, who were as gentle and affectionate as he was. After school or on Saturdays, in good weather, it was a common sight to see the old Emperor with a group of boys and girls, wandering through Chinatown, or down along the docks, or making a tour of the neighborhood firehouses. He was the Pied Piper of San Francisco—only he brought his eager followers safely back from all their excursions.

Loving children as he did, it was only natural that Emperor Norton found Christmas a happy occasion. He knew all the poor youngsters in his vicinity, and somehow managed to have a little present for each

munity no grudge. Quite the contrary; he lost no opportunity to sound its praises as the "Queen City of the World." There were no organized boomers or boosters in his day, but he was in some respects their forerunner. Once a year he put out an "Imperial Invitation" urging everyone to visit San Francisco, and certifying to its "unsurpassable climate" and its "marvellously magnificent Bay." You could always advance yourself in his good graces by praising San Francisco, and sink correspondingly low in them by even its smallest disparagement. Particularly did he resent hearing the City of Saint Francis called "Frisco." "The name is San Fran-cis-co!" he would announce sternly to anyone who in his presence committed this variety of verbal mayhem. And just to keep the record straight—so that all who ran might read—he once issued an "Imperial Proclamation" reading:

> "Whoever after due and proper warning shall be heard to utter the abominable word 'Frisco,' which has no linguistic or other warrant, shall be deemed guilty of a High Misdemeanor, and shall pay into the Imperial Treasury as penalty the sum of twenty-five dollars."

Whether or not this did much for the Imperial Treasury, there are many of us today who fully agree with the old Emperor that "Frisco" has no justification, and that it *is* an abominable word.

Emperor Norton's interest in San Francisco did not stop with prescribing penalties for the mutilation of its mellifluous name. He was incessantly proposing,

himself. For was it not on a certain Fourth of July that he had been "proclaimed Emperor," and had "ascended the throne"?

No July 4th would have been complete without the Emperor. He rode up front in the parade—usually just behind the float bearing the Goddess of Liberty. He sat on the platform at the Opera House during the reading of the Declaration of Independence and while the "Oration of the Day" was being delivered. And he stood at the front of the platform and vigorously beat time during the rendering of the Star Spangled Banner and America. And throughout the day, wherever he went and whatever he did, he never was without a flag in his hand; besides wearing several small ones in his coat lapel and in his hat. Usually he would issue, a week or so in advance, an "Imperial Proclamation," admonishing his subjects to "suspend all work or business whatsoever for the day of July fourth, the day of our empire's nativity as well as of OUR ASCENSION OF THE THRONE, so that we may all foregather and, with fitting ceremonial commemorate this memorable and momentous occasion." The Emperor loved "library language."

* * * *

Although San Francisco had robbed Emperor Norton of all his worldly possessions, he bore the com-

bons and had issued several scathing "Imperial" denunciations of them, declared that his life had been threatened by a "Bourbon seneschal," and demanded a bodyguard. The good-natured Police Chief responded by sending out two rookie patrolmen, who marched up and down conspicuously in front of the Emperor's hotel room for an hour or so—until the Emperor, evidently having forgotten all about the "threat," came out and started off on his customary daily rounds.

After the Police Force, the Fire Department came next in Emperor Norton's affections. "Our Imperial Civil Guard," he called the fire laddies, and during the afternoon or early evening you were pretty sure to see him at one of the Fire Houses; particularly on rainy days. Sometimes he would be reading the papers; sometimes playing a game of chess or checkers; sometimes dozing peacefully in a big chair, in front of the glowing stove. At the Annual Firemen's Ball he invariably appeared in his full regalia; walking directly behind the Mayor in the Grand March. Afterwards, he would go into the buffet, eat a sandwich and drink a glass of Rhine wine, and then go home.

A red-letter day in the life of the Emperor was July 4th. Though born an Englishman, and always professing his enduring respect and warmest affection for "Our dear Cousin, Victoria," as the Emperor of America he felt in duty bound to see that America's birthday was fittingly observed. Besides, he always took the celebration as, in part at least, a tribute to

a fashion. Miss Blank, the "noted leader" from Boston, was thoroughly annoyed and could not quite conceal it, and the audience was in no mood for sustained serious attention. Audience reacted adversely upon the speaker, and speaker unfavorably upon audience; and though Miss Blank, who had come all the way from Boston for this "memorable occasion," finally got through her address, it really didn't quite "come off." As for the unlucky Chairman, when he stood up to dismiss the meeting (and probably to attempt to repair some of the damage he had done), he only succeeded in making bad matters considerably worse. Before he had a chance to utter a word, some wag in the gallery stood up and yelled "Three Cheers for Emperor Norton!" and amid a tumult of laughter the meeting broke up.

The San Francisco Police Force was always close to Emperor Norton's heart. "Our Imperial Constabulary," he called it, and every year until the infirmities of age precluded, he marched at the head of its Annual Parade. Frequently he got out "Imperial Citations of Honour" which he gave to individual members for "valorous conduct," and whenever a new Chief was appointed, he was always present at the ceremonies of induction.

The Police, on their part, reciprocated his affection, and delighted to show him many little kindnesses. The precinct captains kept a special chair for him at their stations, and the patrolmen gave him newspapers, magazines, and cigars. Once, during the Franco-Prussian War, the Emperor, who despised the Bour-

city in the presence of such a "noted leader of the movement"—a certain mannish Miss Blank, of Boston.

Whatever possessed the Chairman to make him do so remains a mystery, but just as he seemed on the point of introducing the "noted leader,"—and the crowd was making ready to applaud—he hesitated, and then, with a wink, announced that he had a pleasant little surprize for the audience. He had noticed, he said, that they had with them Norton I, and he thought it would be nice if the Emperor of America and Protector of Mexico came up on the platform a moment and received the greetings of his "subjects."

The audience was considerably astonished—people looked at each other questioningly—but somebody shouted "three cheers for Emperor Norton," and they were given with a will.

Unfortunately, the well-meaning Chairman had reckoned without his host. The Emperor came up on the platform, and, with many bows, acknowledged the plaudits of his "loyal subjects." But instead of going back to his seat, as the Chairman expected, he proceeded to make a hot three-minute speech *against* woman suffrage; closing it by urging the women of the audience to "go home and mind their children," and setting them an excellent example by stomping down off the platform and out of the hall.

The horrified Chairman, now thoroughly chagrinned by the unhappy turn his little prank had taken, tried his level best to bring order out of chaos. He finally succeeded—after a fashion. But only after

At the time, these were "voices crying in the wilderness." Particularly so in San Francisco, which, with the atmosphere of the Gold Rush lingering, was still predominantly a "man's town." Woman suffrage meetings were few, and far between. Now and then, however, a "big gun" in the movement would be imported from Boston or New York, and for this occasion a good-sized meeting would be drummed up.

Into such a meeting, one Fall evening, walked Norton I. It is quite likely that he was unaware of the purpose of the gathering when he went in. The chances are that he simply happened by the hall during one of his after-supper strolls—"inspecting the Empire" he called such excursions—and, observing the crowd, decided to go in and see what it was all about.

The Emperor was never one to take a back seat, metaphorically or literally. And so, on this occasion, he marched down the aisle to the front of the hall, and from that point of vantage searched out a chair in the first row, a few feet from the speaker's platform.

As was customary, the meeting opened with the audience standing and singing the Star Spangled Banner, and in this ceremony Emperor Norton joined with a will; facing the audience and beating time lustily with his hat. After the national anthem, the Chairman, a local lawyer, made a few preliminary remarks; proclaiming the purpose of the meeting, and bespeaking the pride and gratitude of the whole

Even the hoodlums were silent, and when he asked the audience to repeat the Prayer with him, some of them joined in. For a moment or two after the final "Amen," the Emperor stood silent before a hushed audience. Then he made a little speech of his own—about the virtue of brotherly love; and the necessity of men living amicably together.

Meantime, the sand-lot orator, sensing the changed temper of the crowd, had come down from his rostrum and slipped away. And when the Emperor ended with the declaration that "we are all God's children," and requested the crowd to disperse, it did so quickly, and without dissent.

There were no windows broken in San Francisco's Chinatown that night.

* * * *

Though by no means a misogynist, Emperor Norton was no feminist. Woman's sphere, he held, was the home. And as often as circumstances warranted, he proclaimed his burning opposition to what he called "pants and politics for women."

In his day, of course, the great boon of woman suffrage; of woman Senators, and Congressmen and Cabinet officers, had not been conferred upon America. However, there were signs of its coming. An increasing number of women, and *horribile dictu,* a few men, spent a lot of time publicly demanding that this "enormous crime against womanhood" be expiated, and in painting an alluring picture of the Utopia that woman suffrage and "woman's rights" would promptly usher in.

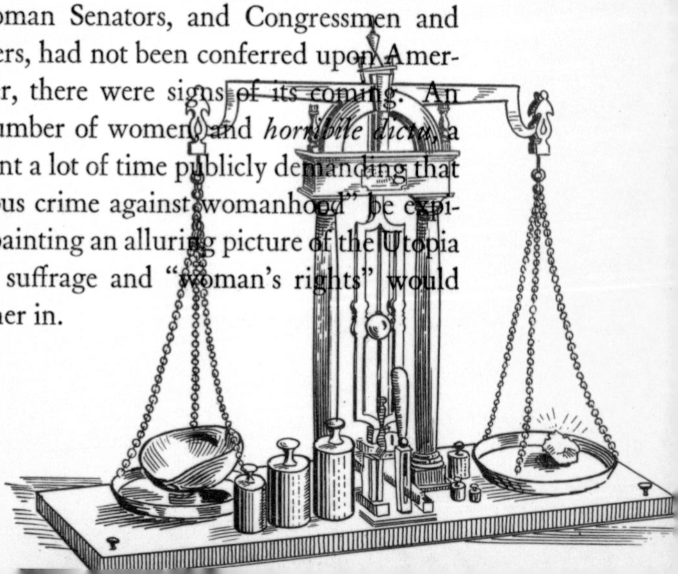

way through the crowd, up to the big packing-case which was serving as a rostrum, he held up his hand for silence.

The speaker, whether momentarily nonplussed by such an unprecedentel interruption, or because he thought that a bit of drollery might not go amiss with the audience, stopped his harangue, and announcing that "we will now have a few words from his Imperial Majesty Norton I, Emperor of America," invited the Emperor to mount the packing-case.

There was a roar of laughter from the crowd as Emperor Norton, with some difficulty, got up on the big box. But the laughter was short-lived. The Emperor, steadying himself with his heavy cane, closed his eyes and commenced reciting the Lord's Prayer.

anity, and of it a contemporary remarked: "It had this advantage over many pretentious theological explications—it contained no un-Christian sentiment."

Broadminded in matters of religion, Emperor Norton was equally so in respect of race. To him, Germans, French, Swedes, Italians, Spanish, Russians, Jews, Gentiles, Irish, English and even the Chinese, were all "God's Children." Accordingly, he was stoutly opposed to the anti-Chinese agitation that went on in San Francisco during part of his "reign." Though not a numerically large element in the city, the Chinese, because they lived clustered in one section and adhered rigidly to their racial customs and conventions, were looked upon as unduly alien, and it was easy to stir up sentiment against them; a pastime in which certain labour leaders of the day specialized; just as labour leaders and politicians of a later date, to further their own ends, stirred up antagonism to the Japanese.

One evening Emperor Norton was out taking his customary after-supper stroll, accompanied by his two faithful dogs, Bummer and Lazarus, when at the corner of Kearny and California Streets he came upon a typical sand-lot anti-Chinese meeting. At the moment the Emperor arrived, the speaker was at the height of his passionate harangue, and the young hoodlums who made up a large part of his audience were cheering him on and voicing their own imprecations of the Chinese.

The Emperor took in the situation immediately, and immediately went into action. Shouldering his

royalty of his cargo, demanded fare. The Emperor was properly outraged. He returned ashore and the same day published a proclamation reading:

> We, Norton I, *Dei Gratia* Emperor of the United States of America and Protector of Mexico, do command that the Steamship Company for denying us a free passage to Sacramento be blocked on the river by the Revenue Cutter, *Shubric,* until the rebels surrender.

The "rebels" surrendered; the steamship company immediately sent the Emperor a letter of apology and a pass on all its boats for life!

* * * *

Although apparently not a member of any church, Emperor Norton was sincerely religious, and as broadminded in matters of religion as in other affairs. There is a record of his having been a member of the Masonic Lodge, but he did not allow that to narrow his religious views. He attended the Catholic as often as any other church. His custom was to make the rounds, going to one church one Sunday, another the next, and so on until he had completed the cycle. Nor was his piety for mere effect. Essentially he was a religious man. Few, if any, of his manifold proclamations were without reference to the Deity, or failed somewhere to sound a religious note; and aside from the newspapers and periodicals, which he read dutifully to keep posted on temporal affairs, the most of his reading is said to have been confined to the Bible. Among his archives, discovered after his death, was one of his letters which had been published in an Eastern paper. It was directed to defining Christi-

whereupon the Emperor repeated his orders. The waiter—a negro, who doubtless had never heard of Norton I—suggested that the Emperor might not have money enough to pay for all this. In the face of such arrogance His Majesty grew violent. He beat the table with his heavy cane, berated the terrified waiter, and in a loud and angry voice announced that if his orders were not obeyed instantly he would revoke the railroad's franchises.

Momentarily, the fate of one of the nation's great continental railway systems hung in the balance. Just then a group of San Franciscans who knew the Emperor entered the diner; and, sensing the situation, instructed the waiter not only to fill the Emperor's order but to bring him champagne and to present the bill to them. The waiter complied, but it was not until the train conductor had come in, and on behalf of the company and himself issued a wordy apology, that the Emperor regained his composure. Afterwards, he desired to share the champagne with his hosts, and to the now joyously obsequious waiter he gave a dollar tip. A few days after this distressing incident the Central Pacific Railroad Company sent the Emperor a life pass, good on any of its California lines, and in all its diners.

On only one other occasion, so far as can be learned, was Emperor Norton's royal authority disputed or his imperial privileges denied. Again he was *en route* to a session of the Legislature. This time he had elected to travel by the Sacramento River steamboat, *Yosemite,* and the captain, evidently unaware of the

him in the Senate Chamber, and during twenty years he seldom missed a session. There he would sit, listening attentively to all that transpired, and taking copious notes in a large black book which had a clasp and lock, and which he would never allow out of his possession. Testifying in this manner to a belief that the legislative branch of the government should be closely watched—he restricted his activity entirely to watching—he showed that his theory of government did not sanction the encroaching of the executive upon the legislative. Only once did he depart from this policy of silent observation. When General Grant was seeking nomination for a third term, the Emperor requested the Legislature to protest. And when the Legislature did not obey, he sent a personal telegram, direct, ordering the General to withdraw from the contest.

Probably few people know that the ignorance of a dining-car waiter threatened the franchises of the great Central Pacific Railroad. The California Legislature was about to convene in Sacramento, and to accommodate the traveling public, the Central Pacific had instituted the startling innovation of a dining-car on its line between San Francisco and the State capital. Emperor Norton, *en route* to perform his Imperial duties at the capital, entered the diner and, as befitted his rank, demanded immediate attention. Clutching a waiter by the arm, he held him fast while he gave orders to bring him French mutton chops, with side orders of various vegetables, fried oysters, and a bottle of Rhine wine. Released, the waiter ignored him;

Early San Francisco Cable Car

though he considered himself, his life adhered to a very simple pattern. For seventeen years he lived in a lodging house on Commercial Street. Each night he paid 50 cents for the same small room. Why he did not rent the room by the month or week—since it was for seventeen years the same one—is one of the many mysteries concerning him that will never be solved. Perhaps—but it is idle to speculate upon the vagaries of royal persons.

While he lived, there is no record of anyone visiting him at his lodgings. After his death reporters went to his room and described it. On the walls were a number of lithographs and photographs of some of his royal equals, including Queen Victoria, Queen Emma of the Sandwich Islands (Hawaii), and Empress Eugenie taken when she was young and fair.

Hanging on one wall was his sabre, with his silk sash and its rich tassel pendants; and on other nails were his hats and chapeaus with vari-coloured feathers. In one corner were a group of walking sticks, fantastically carved and several of them adorned with silver plates on which were engraved his name and Imperial title. In another corner was the huge Chinese umbrella which he sometimes carried on rainy days.

* * * *

If the Emperor's private life was circumscribed, not so was his conception of his public duties. These, among others, included attending the sessions of the California Legislature. It is said that there was a special seat—a large and comfortable chair—reserved for

> Certificates which are secured by all property of the Empire, and will be paid out of my private fortune if necessary, and which I decree shall be accepted everywhere as of the same value as gold coin or currency of the Realm. In the name of God, Amen.

Suitable for framing, the Emperor's certificates gained a wide circulation. Until the great fire of 1906, many were to be seen hanging on the walls of San Francisco offices and homes.

When he wanted small sums of money for his personal needs, Emperor Norton's habit was to present one of his "Imperial Drafts" to an acquaintance, who humored his delusion, and get it cashed. He usually had a considerable quantity of these on hand. The following is a copy of what was long known in San Francisco as "Emperor Norton's scrip":

> "No. 3043—U. S. The Imperial Government of Norton I promises to pay the holder thereof the sum of 50c in the year 1890 with interest at 4% per annum from date, the principal and interest to be convertible at the option of the holder at maturity into 20 year 4% bonds or payable in gold coin.
>
> Given under our Royal Hand and Seal this 8th day of January, 1879.
>
> Norton I—Emperor"

As may be gauged by the denomination of his scrip, the Emperor's wants were very moderate. Emperor

world at large. He read all the papers and the principal periodicals, and let pass no opportunity to aid his subjects, or to importune them in behalf of progress and stability. In the case of emergency he was equal to the demands of the occasion, and never slow to act. It was not surprising, therefore, that when, along in the Fall of 1870, San Francisco was experiencing a period of very hard times, he had the printer strike off several thousand "Treasury Certificates," as a measure of financial relief and protection. They were issued in the denomination of one dollar, and printed on heavy paper in purple ink. They were large—about ten inches square, and each bore a replica of the Emperor's signature and the impress of his seal. The wording of them ran:

> The Amount of One Dollar ($1.00) and Interest will be Converted into 7% Bonds Maturing in the year 1880, and will be paid out by the Agent of my Private Fortune in case that the Government of Norton I does not exist at that time.
>
> NORTON I, EMPEROR OF THE UNITED STATES OF AMERICA AND PROTECTOR OF MEXICO

The issuance of these "Treasury Certificates" was announced by the Emperor in the following proclamation, reflecting alike a deep concern for his subjects' welfare and an earnest desire to aid them:

> We, Norton I, by Grace of God Emperor of the United States of America and Protector of Mexico, being aware of the deplorable conditions affecting finances, and desiring above all to alleviate suffering and afford to all our people a sound and safe security for their savings, have caused to be issued Treasury

triumvirate were known, and entering, continued barking until he had been given a chunk of meat, which he carried at once to his lamed brother.

Toward the end of Norton's reign both dogs died, within a day or two of each other. Inseparable in life, so were they in death. Their bereaved master and friend, the Emperor, had a grave dug for them in a sand-cliff overhanging the waters of San Francisco Bay, near the Cliff House. There, after a funeral attended, it was reported, by "a concourse of San Franciscans on foot and in carriage," the old Emperor's faithful friends and companions were buried side by side.

There is one report that only one of the dogs was buried; that the Emperor had a taxidermist stuff and mount the other, and afterwards presented it to the proprietor of a restaurant where he frequently took his meals. We are inclined, however, to doubt this report; there is no other evidence of favoritism displayed by the Emperor.

The passing of his beloved Bummer and Lazarus was a bereavement from which Emperor Norton long suffered. Those of his subjects privileged to know him intimately said that he spoke often of the two dogs, and never without an air of sadness.

Emperor Norton did not, albeit, allow personal sorrow on this or any other occasion to interfere with public duty. Considerations of self he always put aside, the more fully to study and promote the general welfare. He was indefatigably diligent in keeping abreast of affairs in city, state, nation and the

roundly. Usually this demonstration brought out the proprietor, whose profuse apologies the Emperor accepted graciously. He then took his seat and finished the meal without further complaint. Ofttimes, after dining, he went to the proprietor and inquired if a receipt was desired, invariably receiving the reply, "Never mind, Emperor." More often, however, he rose in a stately manner and stalked out without a word to anyone.

During the most of his reign, the Emperor was seldom seen without his canine escort, Bummer and Lazarus, the two mongrel dogs whose affection for him and for each other was remarkable, and of whose intelligence numerous instances are noted. Once Bummer was lame from some cause and could not get about. Lazarus thereupon visited several of the restaurants or free lunch counters where the famous

display avarice, never known to ask for or take more than enough for his immediate needs. This applied both to money and to goods and wares. When his uniform became worn and shabby, he simply announced through the press that he needed a new one; the money was always forthcoming. Several times one or another of the newspapers donated the whole amount. Once a newspaper collected it by popular subscription; once the Fire Department did likewise, and once the supervisors of the City and County of San Francisco, with discriminating disregard for the strict legal proprieties, voted him a new full dress uniform at the expense of the public treasury. The full dress uniform was made to measure at the order of the Clerk of the Board, and publicly presented to the Emperor amidst much applause from a large attendance of the populace.

* * * *

A less democratic emperor might have kept a royal chef and a retinue of cooks and servitors, and taken his meals in splendid isolation. Not so Norton I. When desire for food overtook him, he merely looked for the hotel or restaurant nearest at hand, and entered. Once inside, however, he became as particular, both in respect of food and service, as Imperial Personages should be. That was one occasion when the Imperial Imperium asserted itself. He commanded the instant attention of everyone in sight, and if either food or service in the slightest manner displeased him, he arose from his seat, pounded the floor violently with his cane or umbrella, and scolded the waiters

States Senator; and precipitated much hearty applause when he stood up in the midst of the candidate's harangue, and, in a loud voice, announced that the candidate need not bother to speak farther; that he, Norton I, would appoint him to the senatorship without further ado.

What a picture the Emperor made on these important occasions! His full uniform consisted of a blue-green tail coat, bright blue trousers with a red band running down the outside of each leg, gold epaulettes (somewhat tarnished), and, to complete the ensemble, a beaver hat in which was fixed a red cockade and a long green ostrich plume. On extra special occasions he carried a sabre (the gift of an admiring San Francisco blacksmith); otherwise only a heavy walking stick or big umbrella. A red rose often adorned his coat lapel, and from the breast pocket of his coat a multi-colored silk handkerchief usually protruded. His shoes, though hardly indicative of royal station, were yet a distinguishing characteristic, and served to proclaim his predilection to put utility and comfort above beauty and rank. The Emperor suffered incessantly from corns, and humored them by puncturing his shoes generously.

The money that Emperor Norton gathered from his subjects in the form of taxes, was used by him to pay room rent, laundry and other smaller bills, and for charity; for he was always most generous to anyone in need. Cigars, tobacco and an occasional glass of liquor, he took in lieu of money for "taxes," and it was remarked of him that he was never known to

ments." Here is further testimony to his sense of fitness and proportion. And if the extra-legality of his tax-gathering forays is stressed, let it be said in extenuation that they erected no towering national debt; imposed no heavy burdens; reduced no subject to penury and drove none to bankruptcy. Usually the amount of a request or demand did not exceed two or three dollars. Only when the state of the royal exchequer required, did he collect as much as ten. Small amounts were acknowledged merely by a word of thanks, but larger sums he honored with a receipt, signed "Norton I, Emperor of the United States of America," and bearing a large gold seal comprising his royal crest.

* * * *

It may be said of Emperor Norton in strictest verity that he was a most democratic ruler. He scorned royal equipage—no coach or carriage for him—walking everywhere. Nor did he surround himself with a host of seneschals or preserve a cold and haughty seclusion. He went everywhere, attended every public function, and, save for groups of children that frequently followed him, and for his two dogs, Bummer and Lazarus, was always unaccompanied. One of his favorite forms of entertainment was a big political meeting. Neighborhood or sectional rallies he did not bother with; but came a big, city-wide meeting with a brass band and plenty of red fire, and he was almost sure to be found occupying a seat well up to the front of the hall. Once, he was even invited to sit upon the platform, at the right hand of the candidate for United

San Francisco Ferry Building around Emperor Norton's time

Emperor Norton solved by proclamations. (And solved them about as well, apparently, as we do now by resolutions.)

One such proclamation, printed on parchment and directed to the perfidy of politicians, is worth reproducing. It read:

> "The Public Officials having again notoriously betrayed the confidence and trust imposed in them by a trusting people; and having shamefully disregarded the public interest and the people's welfare to feather their own nests; now, therefore, We, Norton I, Emperor of America and Protector of Mexico, do hereby order all such Officials to resign forthwith, and do declare their said offices vacant from the date hereof.
>
> Norton I, Emperor"

The matter of whether or not his subjects obeyed such proclamations gave Emperor Norton no concern. Once issued, a proclamation was left to take care of itself, while he turned, appropriately, to other affairs—proof, if proof were needed, that he was both a benign and a wise monarch, possessing the imperial capacity to believe that none would dare disobey a mandate of such exalted source, and if any there was to dare, it was best to ignore such *lese majesty*.

Although he imposed taxes, Emperor Norton did not put his subjects to the expense of maintaining a host of tax-gatherers. He saved expenses by attending to this important matter in person. Of his ordinary subjects he always *requested* the excise, but upon banks and affluent business houses, he served courteous but nonetheless firm *demands;* threatening, in the case of occasional opposition, to "levy attach-

"Norton I, Emperor of the U. S.—San Francisco

Telegram received. Accept my thanks for your interest in behalf of my distressed countrymen. The rent question will be avoided. I only ask for your authority to call on American people for funds to relieve the wants of my countrymen and you can call for subscription on the generous public of your coast and remit to me at your convenience.

Parnell"

There was also a dispatch from Hongkong, China, which being in Chinese characters, could not be deciphered; and a Proclamation on parchment, which ran as follows:

PROCLAMATION

The taxpayer is now feeling the effects of universal suffrage and the American vote: and Whereas; the fraudulent system which the politicians have engendered cannot give the taxpayer his pro-rata of the spoils. NOW, THEREFORE, We Norton I, Deo Gratias, do hereby prohibit the Water Commissioners from signing the Spring Valley Water bill under penalty of decapitation until a sounder system shall have been adopted.

Given under our hand and seal.

(The seal of the foregoing is an especially gaudy one.)

Norton I had a penchant for proclamations—they seemed to give him much the same pleasure and feeling of duty-well-done that we of today derive from passing resolutions. So, whenever a problem troubled him, he went to his printer and got out a proclamation. High water rates, excessive taxes, deficient lighting or sewerage or transportation—all these problems

"

City of Mexico—
via Brownsville (Tex)
November 12th, 1879

Norton I, Emperor of the United States
& Protector of Mexico

Conference adjourned and I am sustained by the people. Present bonds at earliest moment up to $25,-000,000. Your salary fixed at $20,000 per annum, payable quarterly in advance. Draw the first installment through J. J. Murphy, 231 Kearny Street.

Diaz"

There was Norton I's message to John Parnell and Parnell's reply, which read:

"To John Parnell—Irish Agitator:

The Emperor has no objection to your obtaining money to relieve the distress of your countrymen but abolish political and rent agitation in this new country.

Norton I"

endeavouring to secure the Pope's intervention to prevent hostilities, he sent much "good and friendly advice" during the Franco-Prussian War. And upon the success of the Prussian arms in 1872 he caused to be published and placarded about the city a proclamation of rejoicing, which bore his *imprimatur* and official seal, and read:

> We, Norton I, Emperor of the United States of America and Protector of Mexico, do hereby decree and ordain that for the period of one week from and after the date hereof and beginning forthwith, the people shall indulge in continuous rejoicings and most fervent prayers of thanksgiving, for that the God of Hosts, in His Majesty and Wisdom, has lent great prowess to the arms of our friends and blood-cousins the Prussians and led them to immortal victory for the greater glory of God and the Universal Brotherhood of Man. *In hoc signo vinces!*

Further proof that Norton I took his position seriously and that in this he was humoured graciously by the citizens of San Francisco, is to be found in some of the other documents which were found on his person after his death.

There was a cable from Lord Beaconsfield, reading:

> " London, Sept. 18, 1879
>
> H. R. H. Norton I, Emperor of the United States
>
> Entertain U. S. Grant on his arrival at the expense of this government and draw funds through British Consul.
>
> Beaconsfield, P. Minister"

There was a telegram from Porfirio Diaz which stated:

One cable, signed by the Czar of all the Russians, read:

"St. Petersburg
Sept. 26, 1879

Norton I, Emperor of the United States
& Protector of Mexico

We are advised that Queen Victoria will join you in wedlock to bind closer the ties of United States and England. We approve most heartily and congratulate you.

Alexander, Czar of Russia"

Another, from a Cabinet Member of the French Republic, stated:

"Paris, September 26th, 1879

Norton I, Emperor of the United States
& Protector of Mexico

Through diplomatic circles we understand that Queen Victoria will propose marriage to you as a means of uniting England and United States. Consider well and do not accept. No good will come of it.

Grevy—French Republic"

Evidently, Emperor Norton, heeding the latter, "considered well and did not accept." For there is no record of his ever marrying Queen Victoria or of uniting England and the U. S. A. The latter still remains "a consummation to be devoutly wished for" by certain of our citizenry, but the majority seems still disinclined, even after the recent visit of "handsome Anthony" Eden.

Besides Queen Victoria, the Emperor of Austria and the King of Prussia found favour in Emperor Norton's heart. These, too, he spoke of and addressed as his "dear cousins"; and to the latter, after vainly

So far as can be learned, no one, then or thereafter, ever offered seriously to dispute Emperor Norton's imperial position or prerogatives, or to suggest even the slightest curtailment of his liberty. Everyone with whom he came in contact affected to take him and his exalted pretentions at face value—even at the cost sometimes of their own convenience—and treated him with all the show of respect due a reigning monarch. All reports agree that seldom, if ever, did anyone resist his "levies," "taxes" or "assessments," and on such rare occasions as remonstrance was evidenced, it invariably capitulated when gracious requests were superseded by stern, Imperial demands. On his part, the Emperor was temperate, thoughtful and considerate; demeaning himself with the graciousness which indisputable possession of rank and power can afford; yielding to choler and imperious utterance only when strongly provoked by some insubordination or irreverence, and then but momentarily.

Upon "ascending the throne," Emperor Norton I proceeded with commendable dispatch to "establish and declare" his close kinship of blood to certain of the reigning monarchs and royal families of Europe. Being a Bourbon, he had nothing but hatred for Napoleon III, whom he always denounced with great vehemence. Queen Victoria, however, was his "dear cousin," and after his death there was found on his person several cablegrams addressed to him, indicating unmistakably that at one time he was seriously considering marrying Victoria in order thus to unite America and England again.

her because she "longed for his strong government and wisdom," he assumed jurisdiction of this land and people, and added, to his original title, "Protector of Mexico." The "protectorate," however, seems to have been more of an accommodation than anything else. "Beseeched" to do so, he undertook it; but he made reference to it infrequently and his fame partook of it but slightly. For nearly thirty years, until the day he died, his fame rested upon his career as "Emperor" Norton.

When Norton I "ascended the throne" and made public announcement of his investiture with the high powers, titles and prerogatives attaching thereto, it probably provoked no great astonishment amongst his fellow citizens. San Francisco was a swashbuckling sort of place in those pioneer days, where "anything went." It took a good deal to shock or perturb it. But sophisticate that it was, when the new Emperor followed his "ascension" announcement with the declaration that the first duty of the "subjects" of an emperor was to pay tribute; and proceeded to "levy" on these subjects for as much money as his needs required, *that* may have been something of a shock. However, there is no evidence that there was any show of rebellion. On the very day of his ascension, the Emperor is reported to have collected "assessments" totalling upwards of twenty-five dollars from individuals and firms to whom he had been well-known when he was plain J. A. Norton, Merchant, but whom he now treated simply as his "subjects."

his hopes—lay in those ashes. For days he walked the streets—going from one to the other of the places where his buildings had stood; seeing, instead of the comparative wealth they had represented, only sullen, sodden ashes; unable to find solace in the words of any man. His distress was so apparent it was remarked by many—he was well known and well liked in the young community—and when a report circulated that he had been seen several times wandering dejectedly along the waterfront, a group of leading citizens searched him out and offered him financial help to rebuild and restock his store. But he is said to have listened as if not comprehending this kindly offer, "appearing as a man who is dazed and distracted by a deep grief," and, without responding, walked away alone.

Youth soon forgets. Sure of its own rendezvous with destiny, youth cannot give up itself over-long to inaction and vain repining. Soon a new and bigger crop of wooden buildings sprouted in San Francisco, and men had little time to think of their once prosperous fellow-townsman, Joshua Norton. Later, it was subject to comment that he was not seen for many months. Then suddenly, he reappeared. But not as Joshua Abraham Norton, merchant. He returned as a *personage*. He returned proclaiming himself "Norton I, Emperor of the United States of America!"

There is another version of the metamorphosis of the merchant Norton into the Emperor Norton. This holds that the aberration which parented his delusions of grandeur was induced by his financial ruination in

arteries of foot and horse traffic a big, barn-like structure, above which in bold lettering ran the legend, "J. A. Norton, Merchant."

The exact character of the commodities which J. A. Norton merchanted are not set down, but we learn that he was soon "engaged in plying a lively traffic in goods and wares with the miners, cattlemen, sheepherders and other early residents." His traffic must have been lively, indeed, for in less than four years his business had grown to several times its original proportions and he was known throughout the community as very well-to-do, owning besides his store building several other goodly structures in favorable locations.

The beginning of the year 1853 found J. A. Norton a prosperous but plain citizen of the growing city of San Francisco. Who, then, could have foreseen that before the sands of another twelve-month had run out, he would have forsaken the sombre garb and prosaic tasks of a merchant for the habiliments and duties of royalty? Yet that was fate's decree. Toward the end of that year, there was visited upon San Francisco a disastrous conflagration—one of five such that were to sweep the wooden city in the course of a dozen years—and razed it to the ground. Where there had been half a thousand structures of commerce and trade, palpitating with activity, there remained only smoking ashes and ruined hopes.

* * * *

All that J. A. Norton, well-to-do merchant, and property-owner had possessed—the foundation of all

clothe with America's imperial purple, they tell us much, and most of it is charming.

Joshua Abraham Norton, the seventh passenger, was born in London. When he stepped from the deck of the Franziska to the shores of San Francisco he was "about twenty-eight or thirty years old, well built, and bearing himself in the manner of a gentleman." He was wearing a peculiar cape, which "lent dignity to him" and which also, apparently, made him a target for the eyes of everyone. The cape, we learn, was of a "cast of color between blue and red," so that when wet it "gleamed in the sun or lamp-light" and, beginning just atop his heels, reached to his neck, where it ended in a great fur collar that concealed the back of his head and all of his face except his "piercing" eyes and "hawk-like" nose.

At the well-known William Tell House, the principal hostelry of the day, Norton put up, writing his name on the register in a flowing hand, and adding after it the somewhat ambiguous words, "international merchant."

If there was some mystery surrounding the only explanation Joshua Norton gave of what he was, there was not long any regarding what he proposed to do and be. The ink that recorded his name on the register of the William Tell House was barely dry before he was out of the hotel, casting an appraising eye upon the wide expanse of vacant area which the crooked streets carved off. And in less than two months from the time that he stepped ashore from the leaking Franziska, there stood on one of the main

him when he made his kingly rounds; fed him sometimes, and his two dogs; and, now and again—in exchange for his imposing Royal Receipts (printed in purple and bearing the regal seal of gold)—paid money into his "Imperial Treasury."

It costs the gods of high heaven no pains, it seems, to exalt plain men; and as such a plain man Joshua Abraham Norton was born.

He was born in England, and in Imperial England he remained a plain man. It was in America that he was exalted. It was—paradox of paradoxes—republican America that made him *Emperor* Norton!

But to our tale.

Evening of a bleak day in the month of November, 1849, saw the lookout atop Telegraph Hill watching the tiny Dutch schooner, Franziska (or Franzika), showing unmistakable effects of a merciless beating from the storm-swept waters of the Pacific, coming slowly through the Golden Gate and into San Francisco Bay. Part of her cargo had been washed overboard, and she was leaking badly from opened seams. Only the cessation of the storm and a change in the wind two days out of San Francisco, said her master, had saved her from sinking.

Records—those skeletons of cold facts upon which time engrafts layer after layer of the warm flesh of honest man's imaginings, tell us little about six of the seven passengers aboard the Franziska. Nor do we know in what harbor the tiny schooner rested in final anchorage, nor the fate of Nicolas Dau, its stout-hearted captain. But of him whom destiny was to

SAN FRANCISCO'S EMPEROR NORTON

READER, do you know that America had an Emperor?

Had, we said, for he is dead and gone these almost three score years, and only lives today in kindly memory.

Sixty years ago it was not so bad a fate as now to be a king; and Norton I, crowned (by himself) "Emperor of America" and (later) "Protector of Mexico," reigned for more than twenty-five years; reigned until the coming of Age and Death, those twin presences that wait for all Mankind; reigned serenely and beneficently, in unbroken dreams of royal grandeur.

San Francisco was the seat of his Empire. Here he reigned; and among us to this day there yet remains a fastly thinning few who knew him well—saw him as he daily walked the cobbled streets; talked with

Ay, but thou talk'st as if thou wert a king.
Why, so I am, in mind; and that's enough.
But if thou be a king, where is thy crown?
My crown is in my heart, not on my head;
Not deck'd with diamonds and Indian stones,
Nor to be seen: my crown is called content;
A crown it is that seldom kings enjoy.

—Shakespeare (King Henry VI).

San Francisco's

EMPEROR NORTON

The Story of Norton I
Emperor of America
and
Protector of Mexico

By

DAVID WARREN RYDER

First Printing—January, 1939